VIDEOTAPE

V I D E O

Counterpath

TAPE

ANDREW ZAWACKI

Denver 2013

Counterpath
Denver, Colorado
www.counterpathpress.org

Printed in the United States of America

Library of Congress Cataloging-in-Publication Data

Zawacki, Andrew, 1972–
Videotape / Andrew Zawacki.
p. cm.
Includes bibliographical references.
Poems.
ISBN 978-1-933996-34-9
I. Title.
PS3626.A93V53 2013
811'.6—dc23

2012027213

Cover and text design by Michael Flatt.

CONTENTS

for Joshua Harmon & Forrest Gander

They seem within the polisht Grass
A Landskip drawen in Looking-Glass.

ANDREW MARVELL

—edgeless, and partial to nothing—

C.S. GISCOMBE

TRACK A

ERRORMIRROR

II

Grayscale breath on a fluid
field, with lo-fi
rainpatter—petrol blue—,
a 60-watt sun uns
-crewed from the
woebegone sky: [rip-
rap & coal slurries,
dragline & loess, what phosphor
-us is a semaphore
for, silklike
in its acoustic shadows
louver away, or stay
when I move:
figures astray from the mercury
dark—shatterproofless,
shutterproofless,
image noise
stressing each contour to
strass—
as if the margins were
swarming with
centers, or cinders
—"Ecchoes
to the Eye"—
or Cinderella's slipper
blown of poly-
vinyl butyral
& laminated glass

II

Signal glitch is a cut flower
ghost, aghast
in the A/V cable:

Zildjian copper
dapple on the valley
flashing's ½" crimp,

concussions of thunder,
ninjutsu rain,
the terrapin road a rutted

tain & downshifting
into the glare, as if staring
at someone's kyanite

eyes to figure out who
filmed her: moiré
of birch at one edge

of the pasture, canary grass
swaying alarm,
while a Lazar-

us us is us
-hered by the afternoon to
rise, receive the storm

II

To accord the places
their flinty names:
Cassadaga, Cheekto-
waga, Exit
54 to East
Aurora toward West
Seneca,
the Lackawa
-nna coal mine shafts, closed
as Cayuga
is cobalt & Stihl, & all
the painted
pills
that/ fall,
je
-rry-rigged & je
-june, in June,
steeled
within a girder/ of welded
steel: so push
came &
shove came,
fast
from the meadows, the ex-movie-
plex, each raindrop
a prism,
its spectrum
a trick of machine

II

Ripples garbling the play-
back, diagonal & zipper-cinched

—like lightning fitting
a river with Kevlar, its surface

graphing the prelude
to an Indian summer storm,

or blinds that splice a kitchen
window, as windrows

slat the house, & the rifting
of the staircase into splut-

tering video clips—:
automatic elegies,

before evening charcoals
the rooms, for the coffee table,

its Windexblue pane, a
dog-eared magazine,

the orch
-id as it arch
-es toward the sun

II

Land-
fall thru the lens
of a Leica M4:
ball-&-burlap
Japanese maples,
arthritic plaint
of an idling rig,
the platelet clouds
an Arc
-tic upside down & thawing out:

in post-consumer
Pennsylvania
where snow like a
rose knows no
why, a Northern
cardinal—taut
in f/2—is perched
on a larch's branch,
its scarlet not
a quasar but a blur
of opera

II

As if to render a center
peripheral,
we sonared it out of in
-somnia

& branches kvetching
the roof: a midnight
train at 1 in the
morning, hectoring

west to catch its future up;
& later, thru
the crêpe de Chine & EKG
of a fastgelling rain—its

fracas an intercom
on the fritz—*le lever de*
soleil was a radiator
coil inside a cloud

& trees crashing under the
white
wet
weight

II

Uncon-
cern with everything but
care for
every thing:
digraph & lesion, a hy
-phen of ivory
stone, spanning
the mirrored,
the memoir canal,
the wind & where it came
from, warm where it
once awayed,
& waiting at the vaporetto &
turning in
tune with a
hydrocarbon sun:
left
is
right,
right
left

II

On a back road of 'Bamako
la Coquette'

—sunset a Coleman
Pack-Away lantern

its 4 D alkaline
batteries shot—

a little kid tapping
a skinny tire

with a stick,
then he stopped:

kyrielle of bulbuls
bickering

brushfire smoke
from a laterite pit—

I saw
that he was pointing

not
what he was pointing at

II

In the presence & present tension
of some footage got double
exposed: a baobab in the
Luxembourg Gardens, tamarind
grove at the Porte de Pantin,
plastic sacks are loose elastic
tumors in the trees; & fires on the
rice fields, a totaled petrol tanker
as a Tonka truck the mower
struck, galactic orange bonbon
wrappers strewn on the hedges
like asteroid shards, faux Vuitton
& phone cards sheathed in aqua
cellophane: a piazza of faces oc-
cluded by point-&-shoot cameras
is a community, every tourist a
backdrop in someone else's shot

II

The maje
-sty of the image
veils the ramshackle damage
it levers, or laves, awake
inside the sleep its patrons
pay to stay poolside at:
the transparency of the spectacle
's spackle

—etch-a-sketch
billboards, shopping mall,
channel
surfing the nightly
news—

varnishes
as it vanishes via
corridors thru diamond,
thru decimal,
rooms without lintel, nor lock
on the door,
a Quaker gun
strafing the paramour
snow & blowing
its antecedent to
muslin glass: no
longer a language for
a love for what it
it is

II

Constellation selon
les lois du hasard:

a micro volcano
drilled from the deck,

its treated railing
ribboned with rifling

thru pine's raw
underplank, a perfectly

circular puncture
wound, like a stylus

steady in spinning
wax—inverse Vesuvius,

its sawdust lava
frilled by a carpenter
bee

II

Red :: green ::
blue ::
seen as if thru a development
fog, & dropout
as the lightning flares, as
if by aluminum screen,
saturating the view
-er & the view
: a hardhat taking a smoke
break,
ash on a pallet of
sturd-i-floor,
the hiss his
hys-
terical match makes,
flicked beneath the eaves be
-fore per-
cussing his life
to the punch of a staple
gun:
content is nothing
more
than ex-

tension of form

II

Crepuscule
laid in ceramic tile,
portobello & aubergine,
a jet plane follows the fade
to the west
—slowing the sundown down—,
cutting azure
& caulking the azimuth's
cracks: 32,000' above the
mesas, earth is a topo-
graphical map & geodetic
survey of itself—
dental floss rivers, parks
in parquet—scaled to the splay
& manicure of a micro-
chip, or a mother
-board, wrinkled
at the seams &
neuro-
logical in layout, while the 747
surfs, a bullet slacked to
slo-mo
& studied for its trajectory as a
function of headwind &
tacking & hull: that distance, over
the puzzle-piece
ground, assembled from the air is
bared as time

II

Black ice seared
to the corduroy road,

vinca-
dyed by a solstice

moon made aphro
-disiac—"'land'

(the verb) &
'scape' (to

view)"—
ace coming down

the river down
below

II

The canning company ware-
house, leather
& bottle
-works, coffee grindery
billeted in a shite
tobacco shed:
as a cement truck
idles curbside, its barrel
a bullet thru rifling,
tectonic cloud
& blacktop format
-ions
—nitrate plates of each other—
vise a project
Tyvek stucco
-wrapped: & a builder
stiff on the scaffold, stepping—
it would be a long
way, a lasting way
to fall—over
a feng shui medley of
rusted brads, bent
in a block of wood,
by a sheet of tin
the drizzle is starting to bang

II

That things mean by being: our
industrial trash barrel, curbside
at 5, recycling bin with a ziggurat
of Perrier bottles & Dr. Pepper,

prettier for the diffractions of
metal—41ALU upcycled, as sun-
light to scatter the sun—, a
sweepstakes envelope & its gaudy

seal: alone in the real, on good
terms with our neighbors, the
lawnmower stashed in the crawl-
space is safe, but someone's been

filching the A/C units, a tape
deck from out of the car—no, we
like the way it is the way it is, the
way we are: aroused by the chill

yesterday morning, an mp3 of
birds at the sill & clothing pinned
to the line, I lay inside a life
which—for all I know—is mine

II

Magnetic
tape & its

meta-
physics

of lurk &
look

for leaks
within

the negative
cutting

of Zeno's
zones:

bends & snaps
in two

at the lens,
as the uni-

verse
straightens,

estranges
itself

II

Or the dance we do is
Orrery—one around
the other & done—,
widdershins &
wingèd, dizzy, waltzing with
day & with dark: or making love
to a lightning bolt at the arc of
afternoon, her glow-
stick lipstick slick
& licorice

—lowwater, glassscape—

& phoe-
nixed
by her face

as if a trap
door in the trap door
alone might keep a gravity
aright:
you're a Luftwaffe of star
light, shot
thru a subway car,
& I'm nothing
if not all
lit
up

beautiful

II

Cicadas telexing om, om
& twinflower & tomahawk
in Fata
Morgana née South Carolina,
as riffles along the
Riemann surface—blades of
taffeta, soapstone
flensed—of earth the only
ardor toward an earth:
                                        spherical,
sapphirical, drug
from up the lagan
dark to blossom at/ dawn & to
blazon by dusk,
when summertime bobby-
soxes with spring—its
Pyrex glitter of April
showers, chamois
wrinkly or pink de Chanel,
the breakaway
glass of the marriage of May &
morning's kiss 'n'
tell—& the bourbon
crick runs slow beneath a
bridge some
bandit builded out of
dead &
drift & flyspeck brattice wood

II

Whatever is
fastened—fix against flux
—is under assault from the same:
laundromat off the service
road, collision shop,
the tire & wheel, or a boat
on its trailer, its rigging
unhitched, taking
rain &
rusting out the yearlong
in the yard;
if winter's
a prospect of shogun snow,
caulking roof & gutters,
the brick, to stall or still,
distill itself
to the bleak whence the world
began: first,
is what we forgot, then we forget
that we did,
passing the raceway, old fair-
ground enclosures, an air-
strip over that ridge,
route 60 a slushy
PVC pipe, flush with anti-freeze,
sleazed with icicles
sign after
sign: CLEAN FILL WANTED

II

The linear archive invisible, set
to an E-

z listening channel, a
prosthetic repertoire: formatted

to the bandwidth of
a basement session, a split-

screen track, in 8
mm or Beta-

max: a trace
of how it

was & when &
nothing to play it on

II

Outtake: a teakettle
grieving, 8:

30 a.m., in meshbeat
& russet the leaves

on the porch, to clatter
against a cantering wind,

its staves of banter &
blather & schist, with snow en-

cumbered to swab the scenery
clean:

& ice that glisters, is
listened to,

veils & avails itself—
as clamor or flutter,

plosive &
glyph, a sylph

to flaunt stilettos across
the the

-ory of a floor

II

A still shot soaked
in a vascular

loch, tectonic
x-ray of I without

I: be grass that
bristles, thistles

to thresh, a thresh
-old of hunger & linger &

thirst, or a powhite
smudge off kilter,

off camera,
verging on Renaissance

portraiture red
: to rewind the living

daylights, & the dead

II

The surface a sheet of
emerald sheen, caverns of col
lapsing aquarelle: the
re're insides in
side the inside & out
sides in there, too:
pebble, bubble, pellet,
shell, the ropes & oops of H_2O
& tendons & torsions
of river &
waver,
waves of viscous Gallé
glass, the elegance
of violence is a helix
thru a gallium splay
of wetness & of saturated
vacuum, blue or
gray: whatever
is not water is
what water takes its form
& color from
—air, ore, are,
we are, & leaves've collaged a
kaleidoscope on the Soča the
never-the-same:
its condition is to be
without condition

II

Au petit matin
unspooled from its cartridge,
haze filter
fitted, the flutter & wow,
a gobo to cut down on
Luberon lumens
& cyan à la
Cézanne:
the layered
rock of Rousillon—
orange & ochre, *rougeâtre*
& dun—
the crags a seismographic chart
gone gradual under
a graded
sun, its bended boughs of
illusion of season
as if by animation or slide motion
film:
what's moving
while the vineyards
blear & swaths of lavender
liquefy, smear
—zip pan
over the plane trees, ferrous
the paladin
darkness deferred—
is us

II

Are we in an en
-vironment—nowhere we can
be & not be there—or are we
of it:
dried yarrow
& piccolo basil, flaking
from a vase on the sill,
the dishwasher
anthem
—hydraulic falsetto—
biffing & chafing the bone
china plates,
soap on stainless
on stick-proof Tefal & I'm
scared to hell of the fuck if
I know,
that something will
take you, before I can go,
& haul me with it while
leaving
me behind:
a man can unbuckle at
nothing, at night—like a ripple
peeled back

from a blade

II

By this rakish
twilight, its Xeroxed
veneer, a close-
up
veers & loses its locale:
fontanelles
of saline flats,
the fogged
& weft-knit
knot & null,
a piece of floe
in the Genovese gray &
gravel
-level under-
tow:
the way shorebirds at a distance
lease their color before
their shape
& then are lost—accents
from a province out of
colloquy
& hi-res
turquoise
& the cold

II

What rough-cut
lumièresthétique,

what merry-go-
round of the cam-

corder's gaze: subfusc &
wrought by the image,

fumed by
a flashcube burnt

by the view
: klieg lights

thru a window
write a window

on the wall

II

Weather report: oxide clogging
the video head, atmospheres lit
by T-bulb, by tinsel, & carrier
waves getting jammed by a front,
the radio frequency sputtering
infrequent:

a shotgun
shell disch-
arged from its ch-
amber,
steel whisk
dragged on a snare,
what ice
& blistered
fuses would
blare if
ice could
sing if winter
had a larynx
& a zinnia
-scented ling-
o & an I—

II

Like this one— think I'm a fan of the more minimalist ones

Enzeroed by the ozone

in Deskjet scarlet & halogen

white
little apses of renegade

first light, thru the luciferrous

air—then the dark & its

phantom scaffolding

collapse

II

& the knowledge
this will be watched by someone

other than who is now &
here & hearing

this whirr for the first time,
on the further side

of the glass,
& is fastened to a future

forged of after, in de-
fault: virtual,

vicarious, ec-
static

fact embroidered/
-balmed on video/ -tapes-
try

II

Villanelles
of an aniline,
analog tide,
weather balloon
a white
chandelier,
crunch of two
cars in a car
-park punchup,
a Wawa wa
-ter bottle under-
foot: vellum
& wavewoven,
nowherethrown,
the tongue
is a phase 1 SIM
card—portable
tri-band, 64K—,
& salt water
brushing its sutras
on the sand
at the Jersey shore,
in this world
that is not
world enough & is
not not
a world

TRACK B

LUMIÈRETHÈQUE

Country comes from *contra*—opposed: “land spread out over against the observer.” The reservoir cast incarnadine, by the GIF of a cardinal, & clifffall & thawwater, the Alleghenies in gun cotton fog, isleted air pared baby aspirin white. Magnolia flak, at the forest edge, & a burned CD, skipping.

Onion farmers with calabashes, irrigating an emerald plateau. Cf. Fig L-14*a*: "Location is where the camera is." Sunup is affricate, & warm, its grammar a macramé aura on the mirror. Not as quaint as the calendar. A language to lockstep my lung inside, this I I tightrope walk a wire with:

Montparnasse, 8h20, drat light mattes the station sterile. TGV a still life, moving, a "mixture of figure & labor." Windmills fenced in a rapeseed field—an asterisk quartet—are alien vertebrae with airscrew heads. 4-track paddock, park-&-ride: inscape blurs & tatters thru a QuickSnap aperture.

Noises that Skype us, scuff us awake: a moto coughing, donkey next door, the imam at 5 a.m. Muzak of the spheres: electronic tropics with Duracell birds, waves breaking in lullaby from a mobile set to 'nature.' Poltergeist & guttural: to mutter, *là-bas,* as the Niger does—muddied, & with a mouth.

A scarlet tanager, 'olive colored,' is scatting the fence of a farm in D-minor, sun a dartboard of calvados, a dime slotting into the ridge. The vale a wet-gate print of the weather, sad & hyperreal, & flat, the haar is a glacier snarled in the firs—an infantry of edit pulses, broken up by ice: | | | | | |

At ISO 800, at night, Dixie's a garden of bayonet hoods—Nikon HB-35, 72mm, blossoming, black—, as the heavens are pissing a stop bath & borax has grimed the fog, Spanish moss *teintée avec du thé*. Shadows gelded amber, under a damsel moon. A haint is pausing there & the water is wide.

Pointillist, encoded in PAL, sunflowers plait like copper gills against the Haute-Garonne. In my head it is always a season, & the season is never not winter. A hot-air balloon over the houses & fields, an earring of ripstop nylon in the pastel, plaster sky. An arietta: the horizon itself is hovering.

Aspect ratio: 1:85:1: a Polaroid nova divided from its light & the tweeting of jets: “there are no stars in / the metropolitan / area skies / only air traffic.” A bail bond center’s guttering sign—fly-lamp argon, Hawaiiish—, & a clearance sale flogged on Commerce Road: EVERYTHING MUST GO.

Muted by a minor key, the sleet in 4-pin/6-pin firewire: a Venn diagram mars the armor of the water. I'm getting used to it—not getting used to it—, & the upturned leaves of the anise tree. A butte is fogged to phase shift—*neige & verglas : vigilance orange*—, as ringlets on a lake return to lake.

snow, black ice

Wildwood Crest is a Cessna tailing its tag line over the seaside. Along the sand—a description of sound, at 7¾ ips—: a man with a crackling metal detector, its Space Invaders laseresque beeps in sys- & diastole, sweeping the beach as if waving a wand to ward the water off. Or coax it back.

26A :: 27 :: 27A :: the figure in any landscape is the landscape. “Even if we’re on an aircraft,” the scientist says, of B-15, “flying above the iceberg, the iceberg is always above us.” Un crosstalk de thermals, quoi—a blister-pack zero fleeces your face—, & the sidewalks sugared iMac lacquer white.

Little green moon in the smoke detector, crape myrtle a violet fireworks. Acetylene stain of an Ektachrome sky, as squalls enfuchsia the Tarn, & the blowdown peroxides a window, "as much lessness as possible" purling the pane. Vocoding: trees in tunics of calico, & love a city in summer: *enneigée*.

Places named for people named for places somewhere else: a blizzard flecking from histogram cliffs, prairies glossed to palladium print—lilies in italics, the lilacs underlined—at the surreptitious click of a shutter release: clean, apical, meaningless—the staccato of chatter, of esker—& quick.

If it ain't broke, don't fix it—break it. By the blue-film AIRPORT MINIT MARKET, its Plexiglas windows rebar barred & troffer pallor interior, taillights saccade an exit ramp & brogue wind fettles salt from a service road. All'll be made more beautiful for the tourists, including the tourists.

A last-ditch hit of Cipro & the camera not apart from the scene consigned. "What do people expect me to do with my eyes?" TRS-80, 'tis of thee: standard P4 phosphor is a lumièréthique, the sun in plangent, Plantagenet red, threading navy & purple, to black: a knife being sharpened to nothing.

A folded harmonics, the transepts of air, cool in a dimmer-switch sundown, the seraphim shimmer of summer auguring off. Hambone up in the tamaracks, vinyl static of matches in a dive bar box. The center is liquid, lakelike. LUNDI :: 23 VI 08 :: 17:04 :: the world exists to end up on DVD.

TRACK A

GLASSSCAPE

II

There is another world & it
is this one:

screen saver
Appalachians, slowly in a spiral,

canebrake & ninebark Photo
-shopped, swallows scatter

& reconnoiter as feathered
torrent files, & the sky

-line is rainbowed, an LED dis-
play: a glass of malbec

& Marlboros, please, a table by
the window with

a view of the view
of the OMNIMAX sea, not

stuck behind some wanker
with a hooker

in a Hummer
fucking up the Aether at a

drive-up ATM

Faceless, almost fiber-
optic,
to beckon an aria
            back: a scavenger music, its
                      runways & spillways,
                           ligatured carving
aligned to a curve,
& the feedback
loop it seines for a tearing, a
                               standing wave
            flushing the circuit to flam
         in the dream of a shivelighted
peneplain, aristocratic
& odali
-sque
-sque,   or the draft of a
                  quartz, chromatic thing
            deferred: the climate croons
      a requiem with paste-up lindens
            & dot-matrix
birds, fleeing & never finishing
their skitter across the steppe,
            to the dustup hum
        from a jew's harp, hobo tongue
                          & the asymptote,
                                     the qua
                                        -qua
-versal slur of a human heart

II

Luster across
the floorboards—
IP address 79.92.111
.153—, on the other side
of the cloister door: turn
the flood,
the spot light on: you can't see
it because it
's there

II

Haloed by the devil's own downpour: stop motion poplars, in a platinum stutter, the binary code of gravity that pulls them toward the sod & solder their UV programming pushes them from, & the binaural ode of a shutter keeps shuddering, stripping the pane of its weatherproof paint, the whinging of its nickel hinges & syncopated thwacks against the siding inscribing a dialectics of storm: the slow build & the shut-off valve, discrepancy heckling an argument as electric lines frazzle, fizzle to blitz by a crossbow bolt of lightning like some Zeus that Zenith manufactured, recalled on account of a coolant leak, & the reckoning after the wracking of the Rorschach was a porch—

II

The vista comes
back back

-ward,
minus words

or weather outside the dis-
play: inches

toward the present as the pause
is cancelled, crenellated

reels releasing icons & their
cryptic, posthumous code,

a horizontal of dull dimension
choreo-

graphed to laughter
& to lifelike-

nesslessness

II

Within the horizon of gabardine
hills, raku-
fired as if forged in the kiln
of no-count Georgia mid-
July, the trees halloo Tallulah
Gorge, velarium & an event in
themselves, gouged by blunt per
        -sephones of crimson & of green
                                        —gren
                              -ache, wasabi, hen
                         -na, Fanta, ferric, gren
                                        -adine—
& a few miles south
off 328, in Tugaloo State Park,
a beach that shouldn't
be there   is, the lake now
8' low, & fishing lures
& sinkers & bobbers are
snagged on roots of the
oak've eroded, & mica
speckling reddish clay where
one can walk beneath an
orphaned dock
are a trillion mini
miroirs among the mullions
composing, composting the bank,
to show the singular, macular
sun what it looks like—severally

II

The sun a disco ball, a bulb,
clouds a lean-to with least to lean
against:
Aleppo
pine & olive groves in a passage
of helical scan, cypresses ranging
a scruffy
peak
as if hay bale twine were all
that tied them back:
a swimmer
caught
on handheld, her body beneath
the surface writhes
to learn:
water,
like her, goes counter to
the current's pull & in con-
junction
w/

II

One city, one citizen, country
-side, cross-dis
solved with replicas,
nitrogen run
-off & calque:
a bottle tree in the back-
yard
of Warren, the
18-
wheeler with 17 wheels you
shot
in central Australia &
dreamt
in Avignon, on
the finger-
snap road
the sun sheened
over,
color banding the wind
-screen's
safety glass: a quadrature err-
or, or
a comma nicking the lens,
coma
that cast a tail to
trail the traffic—

II

A surfeit
pop-up booking the surface
read as depth in the dead letter
river,
if willows & tea rose
rose against a star within
the silver shallows,
moonlight broom's & shadow's
female's
red & yellow buds: the zinfandel
lull of a late August evening
easing off
the asphalt roads & royal
empress trees, a rain so
rowdy a car alarm
tripped
some bossa nova "Blue Chicory
Summer," to summon these
dimmer odes: rumba rumble
of cubic ice
in a Britvic plastic picnic
cup & crickets akin to the staticky
tsk of a rinky-dink
taxi meter to
measure how
long—how far—
how moneyed how many how
fast—

II

A pair of surveillance
helicopters to

hover overh
-ead,

the dream of pure re-
presentation

—or of deity—
initialed again:

out in the lawn
—a calligrammar of

soggy twigs
& sashayed runoff

mud—a man
measures the a.m.'s

advance in 30
-gallon bio-

degradable bags of
longleaf pine straw,

of sallow
soon-to-be grass

II

The radiosilent,
kinescope eye, at

large in some Uffizi
of the laddered,

folding heart—

"I was actually quite happy when
the house was buried in snow,"
the state electricity service rep
said, "because then I wasn't
afraid of the windows breaking"

—a love erased, recorded over,

the flecks still flicker
decay, on a VDT

with a tube blown, black
inside the box,

each shadow throwing a shadow
of its own

II

Fog along the Lj
ublj
anica, gunsmoke to choke
a corral:
the butcher's bridge the
shoemaker's
bridge, their boxes of ruby
geranium buds & satin
refošk in a sable bottle,
a jazz quartet
on a candlelit barge & weeping
willow washer
women, pumicing
the sounded banks to primness
at onset of night, its
Lite-Brite stars
a vernissage a
glow above the glam:
my far &
fallaway sh
adowsh
ekinah—I
will try to sh
ield you from the sh
ards of bulbs the sh
attered
asters
are

II

O hell
o to our micro catastro
phes & Mc
dystopiads: the car not
where we left it in the
airport parking lot, a forgotten
PIN code (48
something),
batteries sapped in the i
Pod shuffle, making
the melody muffle
& scuff, the chick upstairs wears
heels in the morning getting
ready to work it
at work, & the wi-fi
network is flailing
again, the RER B ta da is back on
strike—but I'm far a
way on Cloudfuckyouland
where the weather
is prefab, pay-by-the-
hour, recycles at
5¢ a pop,
& I'm not coming
down until I'
ve rode a gaffer's zephyr
to the tune of to
the tippy Tupperware top

II

A flag in the front yard, fence
at the back, a graphite-
lacquered cat that keeps
appearing on the devilgravel
path: this is our neighbor
-hood aria, our community's
April aporia, a mailbox
bent at a bend in the road,
its tiny red pennant still
up, up, & lindens
nudging the shingles
to jangle, coffee gone flat
in a Styrofoam cup,
as the pixels divide like
pack ice—one part threshing,
two parts thrall—gray
& greenish pink & flashing:
global capital 's local
cater-
waul

II

North of the city there's
weather:
the landing strip lights
in the gloaming, in
bloom
—electric Carolina jasmine,
sego lily
of high-voltage
valley—
& ghostmatter oozing
fluid off the aileron,
the wing,
as if a cloud
had snagged on the Boeing
chassis
—designed
to withstand up to
25 gs but tested
at 2.2—,
its skid marks a text
over avian
time, a piece of the firmament
talon-torn,
sheared by splints of air:
some illluck
god & misbegot that
took its arabesque to
bury there

II

—or the word with
-out a language/
a ligature
sound-/
surrounding its sing
-le event, like a chain
saw loose in some angel's
mouth, teething a wound in the
structure/ the suture, as a storm
on the other side of the sea de-
gausses the grimy
sky of its raster
lines drawn nimb &
cirr & cumul
-us:
o wave
that wrecked against all
grammar, at first light a-
long the Ligurian
coast, & cracked
the fractal windows in
the process/ as
the process:
thank you I
love
you I needed the
brine of/ a breath of fresh
error—

II

Dice
toss
& damsel
in di
-stress:
a freight train
over the rail-
way
trestle,
its axles
darning the parallel
at its vanishing
point, tuppenny tats,
a sunsquall
lolling the trollop
sky
to
blankness
on a VHS cass-
ette—plastic, ballistic—
a vicarage of muting &
of warp where
ever it
was

II

Cell tower beacon a red
boutonniere—

Sanankoroba
on the hook with Sénanque—

& flourishing thru this gunite,
perishing world:

a freesia fitted with
aerofoils

that turn in the wind
& turn the wind

to kilowatt-hours to
power the flower

forth—

II

Itin-
errant impasse
-nger,
pace car
stuck in a Petri dish, what
is it if
not gravity that brazes
the gloaming to you,
a fake Bal-
bec at the
back of the
brain, at rest at the
speed of our do-see-do sun,
& how many billet-doux
have you writ, how
many bullets un-
loaded, or bit,
out here along this old
wreckoner's route,
turning
round a turning
cage, like a cubist
Rubik's Cube?
"That dough I
blew on slow
horses," you say, "they
rolled me for the diamond
& the gun"

Thru weathered glass
& firebreak,

like a Lego-brick
heart with an artery

blocked, the halyard
of rerecording is severed

again: a voice-
over over

-dubbed, weirding the airwaves
with warble & offal:

```
1Ø OPEN 4,4: FOR I = 1 TO 4
2Ø PRINT#4,"THIS IS LINE #
    "I:NEXT I
3Ø CLOSE4:OPEN4,4,1
4Ø FOR I = 1 TO 4
```

II

Verona inside
the body, the

veins, & Venice
dissolved in the mind,

spooling at speeds
of incommensurate order:

a bullet
train crossing a backgammon

board, the metro
to fit inside *un plan*

du métro: help me,
someone says,

take off my face

II

Begins in interruption:
an ambulance bell at the center

of sleep, the room tilts
sideways, furniture slides,

an octet of amber blue
verres à liqueur, one with a cut

at the lip, clatters as a quaalude
light in tatters mattes the

curtains ormolu:
I miss you

is what I want to say
like a rocket

stocked from the Reagan
years, its radar gone haywire,

wiring fried but
live inside a bunker of some

private Soviet
Union you & I—

II

Iris in, iris
out, Sundays
til the sun go down,

lit by inky
dink & snoot—
the bit parts we play

in our layaway lives,
on hands & knees
on the gravel

walk, beating back the
weeds before they
're back

II

Dispetaled & half
awander among the cordura,

Cyrillic trees: chinaberry,
loblolly,

verawood with its
glamorous shrapnel, its

fretwire
canopies drilled to the dusk,

frames replacing frames:
in the bruised, metallic

sancerre light
re- & de-

flected by freshwater
evidence:

a cinematic, a harmonium blue,
smyth-

sewn with orange hydrangea
titles letter-

pressed

II

The transcripts of rococo &
ROY G BIV:
cinnabar, madder,
Moscow, Tiepolo, hawthorn

berries wetted with winter,
the meter
maid's mittens, her
épée of chalk, a goshawk

bitmapping Bi-Lo
—a kite—

relayed by
satellite, 0s & 1s,

to a city shook up in a
snow globe minus
the shaking
& the snows: goodbye, Marx

adieu, Coca-Cola, we're macro
Radio
headheads & mini ex Max
Headroomheads we

put our
money where our mortgage is

II

Each forgery flinted with bezel's
array is a pillar to every-
thing else: this arch
had to relay
the means
of its making
with it as it arose,
chose   a creeper derrick
sidling up the siding under a
riverine sun, the posh & polished
deltas belayed by patience, by
pulleys, by PDM—as I touch
what metal had chilled the
palms of men whose
hands my grandpa
mighta shook:
winched at
80 lbs. of pull,
pipe-cleaner tendons
thru concrete, cement em
-bedded in stainless steel, tack
-welded plates a taut parabola—
plissé of gravity, balance's
torque, the swaying
of poise per
se

II

—an RSS feed of
swallow
song,
dreck light on
the canti-
levered,
errormirror lake—

II

Voices out of sync
with the film,

Carrera green & Duomo
rose, in loggias

echoes ricochet
along: the scratchy

foreground, a faded detail,
the past gutters past

in a present to pass:
the dead brought back

as a screen on a screen—frost
flowers, the candy floss

garden—where death is
not

yet & yes
-teryear's

II

Viewfinder in the vehicle—
motion
picture, moving
car—churning
thru a tunnel thru
a tunnel,
as a sadness
is drawn with the tide's drawl,
peregrine & pebble
s' ebb, thrawn
by the weight of so much
water thrashing
—how many throes—
& whispers at you to s-
wear it until, worn, it wear
-s you
-r inside
-s inside
out—

II

Idiot bleat
of a cipher under

a murmur
below a furor fizzling

mum: teeth
grovel clock

-wise—having
the experience later

once it's over to
file

away &
remember—

& flailing like a strip-
-ped screw:

exit music
for who is not
exiting

II

Motion away from
the spectacle
the spectral
moves with you:
on the piste from Douentza to
Timbuk-
tu two
4 x 4s
are ants along a ledge

II

Snowwork
        & a CGI of blue cineraria,
as if on an un

-inhabited plane:
        vanadium clouds
thru fiberglass passages,

forests of Freon, their
        rheostat trees, branches
Akzidenz

Grotesk to skiffle
        the telecom, tar paper
leaves, the lake

infernal method-made
        by ice & kick-your-ass
northwesterlies: as nitric

nightfall scours the clearing
        —air the event horizon
of air—I see everything

disappearing,
        & there is no elsew-
here here

TRACK B

ZEROGARDEN

The center equals all asides aside. “Local television claimed that activists threw smoke bombs at the police, but what they videotaped was activists lobbing back the tear gas canisters that had been fired at us.” Plectrum leaves, wind-plucked, moog inside the storm: the world is a Wardian case.

This is how it's going to go down: grain silos & mega grids, slingshots dot the Susquehanna, stringing the phone lines in sine wave & synapse, starter castles splatter a forest, newmown grass in lawnbrite hypergreen. Exit wound: gallop wire to the foosball rink, & a grove of bucket trucks off 81.

Nail gun in the nearing night & "faux para-snowfoam." Tower cranes swivel in syncope—gamma 1, gamma 2—as street lamps scribble Farsi on the floor. As if light were only the manifestation of light. Sky now celadon, now sauterne—24" plasma display—& SRS airbags inflating over the kirk.

Locust buzz of a scuzzy lamp, in a Budget parking lot: the syntax of where I stand is where I stand. The evergreens, in Pennsylvania, are gray beneath the Eveready sun. Petals are pleats of staurolite, palaces of wind. An olivier sways in a fickle breeze, as if snow flurried up from the ground.

Rhizome of a railway thru the Bordeaux countryside: to speak is a federal blue Prince Rupert's drop. Tryst of two automated ticket machines, scansion of a hole inside the whole. Frost by fax, a dial-up eclipse, & silver halides lifted by a fixer flurry that dervishes the lake: are never exposed.

Dawn a Saran wrap rapture of pink, in broken correction ribbon ca. Olivetti Lettera 22. "We don't have manpower. We have to do alone with little handicams." The Amtrack track is Frankensteinish stitching past the putt-putt course—& I a caisson, inside which I. "That really happened."

Just off the Jersey Turnpike, ranging the waterway: Maersk containers stacked like butter sticks. A semi sidewinders the passing lane, its tire clacks shivaree our kid to sleep. The windshield set on 'landscape view,' gussied up in gray, & gas is $2.79 9/10/gallon. Chekhov's last words were German.

Data file recovery complete: telephone cables arranged in cedilla, icicles *accent aigu*. A light meter teeter-totters—overcast, the selenium shot—like a spirit level bubble, wavering. Shannon, Reykjavik, Santa Maria, on HF radio, U- or V-: "the night-ark / adrift, / & water- / divided, the / stars."

Rafter solder, medieval vitrine: the vaults of Paddington Station are a Franz Kline calligraph. "I remember that month of January in Tokyo," the narrator says, "or rather I remember the images I filmed of the month of January in Tokyo." Rain quires & giclée clay, in salt-&-pepper motif.

A black & white man on a stepladder, leaning forward to paint his leaning shadow on a wall. Canter of rain on the cobbled walks, the damascene sky is a lantern slide, clouds a collodion positive on glass. Today I planted four cranial bulbs—"*tulipe en turc : petit turban*"—in silver illy decaf canisters.

The surface, say, is fricative—"into clear air a roughness"—, sundown London telephone cabin red. Or the surface is fictive, frictionless: landslips of midnight, & will-o'-the-wisp, a spazzing out of sparrows, at dawn, "through idea-like-snows-through-snows." What is the world. What isn't.

A pop-can skyline with BB holes, its neon swarming, corona of shale, smog
a lye that squeegees the city in streaks. The center, *ici*, is elsewhere's edge.
Neg#AL7-7202: droplets rivet a loading dock like chandeliers cut loose, &
a pencil of menthol cigarette smoke: a bastard genie crashing into the fray.

Nonontology: birches a cello glass to the pasture, lake lit *yttrium*. "One thinks of an image made in the image & likeness of images." Or the frozen sun, its pas de basque, its ruined passageways. Abjad scripture of contrail & distrail, the planet is enhaloed with holes: andscape, endscape, in-, e-.

The borrow pond is frozen over—its flat-screen water, its silkaline limit—
as wrinkles cinch a paper folding fan. Rapier light & mimeo snow, slide-
guitar catharsis of a February dusk. (Galerie K. Greve. Ed. 1/10. 42,000€.)
In the frame of a Sony portable cam, I is everything that is not the case.

A viewer is never not turned away from someone, somewhere else: focus of a separate inquiry. Sun on the shoals: amaranthine. The Jezebel trees tall, treeesque. Throw is the distance an image appears, that light will illumine an object. "If only I could see a landscape as it is when I am not there."

33°5'16"N 83°14'0"W: fluorspar twilight, airbrushed air, kir red confetti of the robins in bacchanal. Rain pitters an r-f pattern—the Altamaha a crawl title in gold leaf tesserae—, & scrolling out from quinol clouds, by zoetrope or strobe: the moon, a strip of aluminum foil, stuck to the film stock—here

NOTES

The epigraphs are from "Upon Appleton House, to my Lord Fairfax" (1651) and "Mnemonic Geography" ("Inland"), *Prairie Style* (2008), respectively.

Track A
Marvell. Painted wood relief, Hans Arp (ca. 1930). Santu Mofokeng, "chasseur d'ombres : 30 ans d'essais photographiques," Jeu de Paume (24 mai au 25 septembre 2011). Andrej Zdravič's soundfilms "Riverglass: A River Ballet in Four Seasons" (1997) and "Water Waves" (1992).

Track B
Raymond Williams, Appendix, *The Country and the City* (1973). Eli L. Levitan, *An Alphabetical Guide to Motion Picture, Television, and Videotape Production* (1970). Roland Barthes, "Sade II," *Sade/Fourier/Loyola* (1971), tr. Richard Miller. Sally Mann, *Deep South* #43 (1998). Douglas MacAyeal, McMurdo Station Glaciologist, in Werner Herzog's *Encounters at the End of the World* (2007). Ed Roberson, "This Week's Concerts" VI ("Lucid Interval As Integral Music"), *Voices Cast Out to Talk Us In* (1995). Hervé (VR99), in Agnès Varda's *Les Glaneurs et la Glaneuse* (2000): "le plus possible de moins." Guy Debord, *Commentaires sur la société du spectacle* XVII (1988): "Tout sera en somme plus beau qu'avant, pour être photographié par des touristes." Giuliana, played by Monica Vitti, in Michelangelo Antonioni's *Deserto Rosso* (1964). Gary Snyder, "Japan First Time Around" 7: VI ('56), *Earth House Hold: Technical Notes & Queries To Fellow Dharma Revolutionaries* (1969). Reporter's voiceover in Anders Østergaard's *Burma VJ: Reporting from a Closed Country* (2009). Evelyn Reilly, "Bear.Mea(e)t.Polystyrene," *Styrofoam* (2009).

Track A

Pound's "Walking Tour 1912" notebooks, ed. Richard Sieburth as *A Walking Tour in Southern France: Ezra Pound Among the Troubadours* (1992). Magndís Alexandersdóttir, quoted in Roni Horn, *Weather Reports You* (2007). Nick Cochran, played by Robert Mitchum, in Josef von Sternberg's *Macao* (1952). "Sample Tab Program # 1," *VK – 460G: A Centronics Parallel Printer Interface with Graphics for the VIC-20™ and C-64™ Computer* (Videoking Electronics Co., Ltd., undated). Gillian Conoley, "[Schools of Thought]," *The Plot Genie* (2009).

Track B

Rebecca Solnit, "Fragments of the Future: The FTAA in Miami," *Storming the Gates of Paradise: Landscapes for Politics* (2007). Karin Lessing, "The Night-Ark" ("The Night-Ark"), *In the Aviary of Voices* (2001). Chris Marker, *Sans Soleil* (1983). André Kertész, *Painting his shadow* (1927). Gérard Macé, "Absentes de tout bouquet," *Promesse, tour et prestige* (2009). Gennady Aygi, "Oakwood and (Across the Field) Oakwood" ("Field-Russia: Part Two") and "Dreams – with Faces of Old" ("Field-Russia: Part Three"), *Field-Russia*, tr. Peter France (2007). Don DeLillo, *Americana* (1971). Simone Weil, *Gravity and Grace* (1947), tr. Arthur Wills.

ACKNOWLEDGMENTS

My gratitude to The Bogliasco Foundation for a residency at The Liguria Study Center, where this project began; the Jane and Harry Willson Center for Humanities and Arts at the University of Georgia, for a grant that allowed me to continue writing; and *Le programme de résidences internationales Ville de Paris / Institut Français aux Récollets*, for a fellowship to complete this book.

MAIRIE DE PARIS INSTITUT FRANÇAIS

Thank you to the following journals and their poetry editors, for publishing outtakes—often in alternate versions or bearing provisional titles: *751 Magazine* (Kevin Weidner and Tony DeCarli), Academy of American Poets' Poem-A-Day series, Poets.org (Hanna Andrews), *The Allegheny Review* (Christopher Bakken), *Antennae* (Jesse Seldess), *Black Warrior Review* (Melissa Hull), *Blue Letter* (Chris Hosea and Cecily Iddings), *Bombay Gin* (Kelly Sexton), *Boston Review* (Timothy Donnelly), *Cannot Exist* (Andy Gricevich), *Cellpoems* (Chris Shannon and Eric Smith), *Chicago Review* (Joshua Adams and Michael Hansen), *Colorado Review* (Sasha Steensen), *Conjunctions* (Bradford Morrow), *Eleven Eleven* (Hugh Behm-Steinberg), *English Language Notes* (Julie Carr), *Hambone* (Nathaniel Mackey), *Mandorla: New Writing from the Americas* (Kristin Dykstra and Roberto Tejada), *The Nation* (Peter Gizzi), *New American Writing* (Maxine Chernoff and Paul Hoover), *The Offending Adam* (Andrew Wessels), *Parthenon West Review* (Chad Sweeney and David Holler), *Ping • Pong* (Jim Maughn), *Poetry Northwest* (Kevin Craft), *Poetry Salzburg Review* (James Cummins, Fergal Gaynor and Trevor Joyce), *RealPoetik* (Lily Brown and Claire Becker), *Second Mind* (Brian Lucas and Brian Strang), *Sentence: A Journal of Prose Poetics* (Richard Deming), *Sous Rature* (Cara Benson), *Vacarme* (Suzanne Doppelt), *The Winter Anthology* (Michael Rutherglen), and *With + Stand* (Dan Thomas-Glass).

Thanks to Claire Sammons and Corwin Peck, for producing a letterpress, hand-sewn, limited edition of *Videotape* with Particular Press (2009).

To Justin Runge, editor of Blue Hour Press, for publishing the digital chapbook *Lumièrethèque* (2009).

To Samuel Amadon and Stephanie Anderson, editors of Projective Industries, for the chapbook *Glassscape* (2010).

Sara Parkel, for a limited edition *Zerogarden* at Filter Press (2011).

Mark Irwin and Andrew Wessels, for including a clip in their Proem Press anthology *13 Younger Contemporary American Poets* (2010).

Jennifer Tomaloff, for inclusion in the online *Bending Light Into Verse*, volume III (2012).

Thank you, Brian Henry, Julie Carr, Forrest Gander, Joshua Harmon, Andrew Joron, Donna Stonecipher, Nathaniel Mackey, Sika Fakambi, Judith Bishop, and Joe Ross, for looking at and listening to this manuscript, with and against the grain.

Sandrine and Ella: *pas de photo*.